the thing

A young boy's journey with Asperger Syndrome

...for Leo and Ben

Authors note:

Welcome to our story. This is only the beginning.
There is a long way to go and I suspect our path will be winding...as will
yours.

When we began this journey I thought I knew what Autism was
       – I researched it for my Psychology degree at University.

I thought I was good at handling tough emotions
       – I train leaders and managers in Emotional
Intelligence and Resilience for a living.

I had never met The Thing.

I have learned more in the last 7 years than in all my years of study and
work,....and realised how little I still know.

There are many amazing books to describe Autism Spectrum Disorders
to children who are either on the spectrum, or not on the spectrum
       – or who don't yet know.

My son doesn't care about what Autism is...

       ...he cares about who HE is.

That is why I wrote this story.

Once upon a not that long ago, there was a boy.

It <u>could</u> have been a girl...

....but it wasn't.

It was a boy.

This boy was special.

Not more special than his brother.

Not more special than other boys
for that matter...

...but special nonetheless.

What, I hear you ask, was special about this boy?

Well...

...this boy had

a THING!!!

The Thing was called ASD, Asperger's or Autism by the big people.

But to the boy...

...it was just a Thing.

Thing! ↗

Sometimes he could forget completely that he had this thing...and so could the big people.

When they forgot, they would treat him just like any other boy.

They would take him to parties and let him eat sugary treats...

...and bounce on the bouncy castle like all the other boys and girls.

They would let him wrestle on the sofa
with his brother...

...or take him to their friend's houses

and <u>only</u> talk about big people stuff

– not The Thing.

They would even take him on whizzy fairground rides...

...and on an aeroplane...

on holiday...

to France!

Sometimes these things would go OK...or even really well.

He would get that buzzy feeling that happened when he drank fizzy drinks...

...and he would want to cuddle everyone in the whole world.

The big people would be really happy...

...and so would the boy.

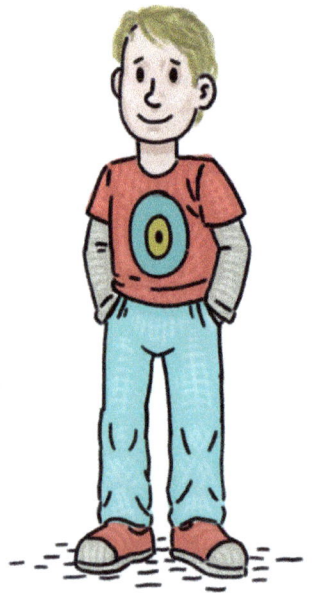

But sometimes they didn't go so well...

...because half way through doing them the THING would appear.

The boy couldn't control the Thing very easily at first.

It made him
feel dizzy and
want to spin...

....and his head
go all busy
and messy.

It made his
tummy go all
bubbly inside...

His ears
would sound
too loud...and
his eyes would
stop seeing...

...or everything would be
too bright, or too fast,
...or too complicated.

When the THING appeared,
the boy would sometimes do
things he didn't mean to.

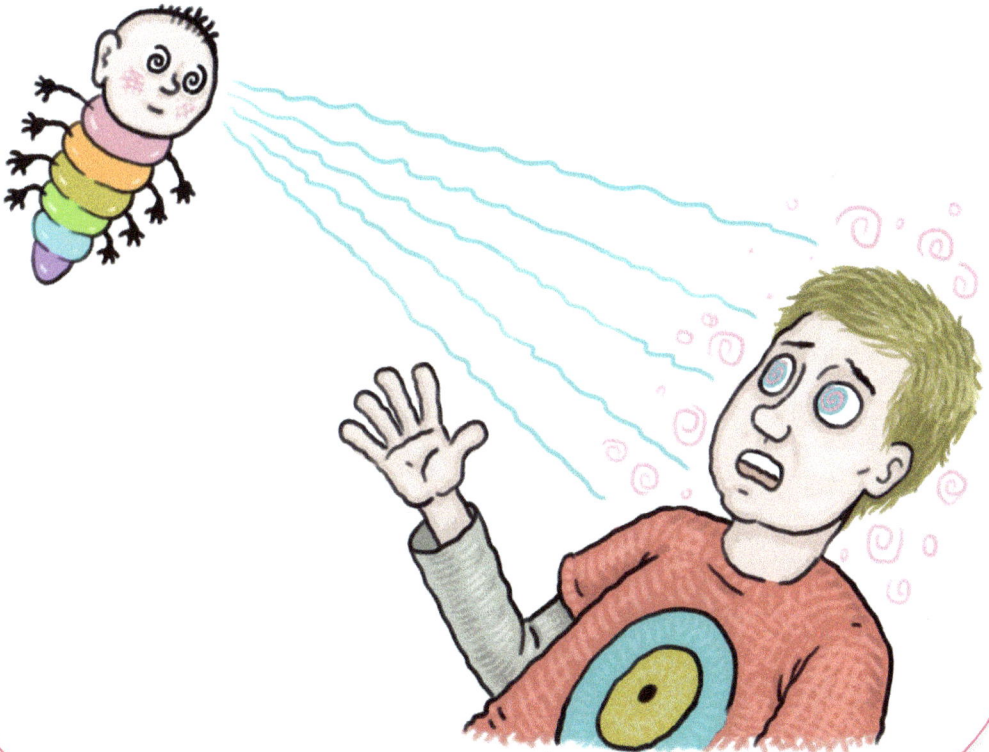

He might flap about or
bump into things...

He might make odd noises
that other people said
hurt their ears...

He might even run away
– or hide...

...or hurt the people he loved
by biting or hitting.

When these things happened it made him sad and afraid

– and when he felt those things all he wanted to do was to run or fight...

...or hold onto people for longer or tighter than they wanted.

He tried to stop...but it was hard.

When these things happened
<u>everyone</u> remembered that
the boy had the Thing.

They talked about it a lot...

They seemed worried, or upset...

...or sometimes really cross.

The boy sometimes felt that
the Thing was bigger than him.

But sometimes, just sometimes, the Thing would do AMAZING stuff!

Sometimes it would make the boy remember all the words to his dad's favourite songs.

Sometimes it would make him notice how beautiful the clouds were ...and see dragons and castles in them.

It would make him create the most incredible spaceships out of Lego
   ...and be able to tell his mum exactly how they flew and fought the bad guys.

Sometimes the Thing filled the boy's heart and made him say the most wonderful things to the people around him...

...but only sometimes

...and this made the boy sad.

Why did the Thing not let out
those nice things inside him all
the time?

Why did feeling either sad or
happy make him do things
that other people didn't like?

As the boy grew older the Thing often
made him feel lonely

...or really angry.

He watched the other kids play together.

He tried to join in...

...but somehow he did all the wrong things and they laughed at him ...or ran away.

How did they know what to do
or what to say?

It was as if they had no Thing
to worry about.

But he did...

Although some days he could keep the Thing behind him, or inside him....

... other days he couldn't be himself at all.

It shouted when he wanted to be quiet.

It ran and spun when he wanted to walk and watch.

It hid all his words so he couldn't find them.

He started to be afraid of the Thing.

One day a lady came to visit the boy.

She told him she knew
about the Thing.

She wanted to see what it
looked like and how it worked.

She didn't seem to want to hide it or make it go away

– only to understand it.

She taught him things he could do to feel stronger.

Over time she,
and other people,
helped the boy to see…

….that he wasn't the only person
who had a Thing.

...in fact everyone around him had at least a little bit of one.

They weren't always obvious...

....and his was just different – not more... not less.

One day, the boy decided to have a
chat with the Thing.

He reminded the Thing that it wasn't
the biggest after all.

Every day *he* got bigger

...and bigger...

...and the Thing just stayed the same size.

Every year, although the Thing never went away,

...he was less afraid of it.

Soon he would be able to choose whether he
did the nice things
        ...or the things that made him
feel lonely or angry....

...he would be able to choose whether he held
the Thing inside
        ...or shared it with others.

The Thing would only ever be a THING.

And he...

...he would always be a boy

...and he would _always_ be special.

Parent / Carers Notes:

This book is designed to be read s l o w l y with your child and to be an interactive experience

> – in whatever way it works with your child.

The Thing personifies what ASD *might* look like for <u>one</u> child...your child's Thing may be different...and that's OK

Start a conversation with your child about what it might look, sound or feel like to them.

What does the Thing do that makes them happy or sad?

Their thoughts, language and descriptions may not make sense to you and may not be consistent

> ...but the conversation is what matters.

We are acknowledging that there are parts of the child that sometimes don't feel OK

> ...and that is true for all of us.

You may even want to share parts of you that you sometimes struggle with. This connection is important.

When your child changes the subject...let it go.
> It's time to move on and they may need time to process the story.

You may mention The Thing in passing later on and find that it has become something open to exploration

> ...or you may not. Either is fine.

When I read this story to my son, he was very clear that his Thing was red when it was doing things he didn't want it to, and green when it was being good...fair enough!

Use the space below to capture The Thing for *your* child – and **let them lead**. The Thing might be scary for them...or sad...be large or small, red or black. It may change shape or colour for different reasons...or it may not have a shape at all!

Classroom ideas:

When presenting this story, try to read it out loud but stop to share the pictures with the children on each page – encouraging discussion of their own experiences.

It is important that every child's particular perspective on the Thing be respected

– **we are <u>all</u> different.**

There is an opportunity for <u>all</u> children to relate to The Thing as the boy in the story does.
This does not need to be a targeted discussion about Autism or ASD
– but about parts of ourselves that we struggle with
at times but are learning to manage.

- Ask the children to think about how it might feel to struggle with things that others seem to find easy.

- Open up a discussion about what we might do to help others feeling this way...and explore how maybe the *way* in which we help might need to be different.

- Encourage all the children to draw a picture of what their Thing might look like; what it might do. Ask them how they feel about it.

About the Author:

Rachel studied Psychology at Royal Holloway University of London before training in counselling, coaching and NLP. She worked for 6 years in London as management consultant and went self employed in 2007 with a view to shifting her own work-life balance.

Whilst travelling independently around South East Asia she met her South African partner, Brad and they settled where Rachel grew up in rural Suffolk.

Rachel is now the mother of two boys – Leo (7½) and Ben (5¾). She balances her own coaching, facilitation and leadership development company – Changing Dialogues Ltd with the challenges of bringing up a family.

Leo was diagnosed in 2015 with High Functioning Asperger's. At risk of exclusion from successive local primary schools he has been welcomed for over two years in a fabulous Pupil Referral Unit near his home.
Now taking daily taxi-treks to attend school in Cambridge....the nearest facility equipped for academically able autistic children with behavioural issues, Leo is just beginning the next phase in his own journey with Asperger's.

Rachel dedicates this book with love to all the incredible friends, family, teachers, support workers and complete strangers who have helped both her and her family on this extraordinary journey.

Rachel...has her own thing!

Find out more about Rachel's 'day-job' at www.changingdialogues.com

About the Illustrator:

Zeke Clough is an illustrator based in Todmorden, best known...so far...for his distinctive sleeve artwork for electronic musicians such as Shackleton and Ekoplekz. His partner of eight years has 14 year old autistic twins who go to a specialist communication school.

Zeke's love of comic strips and drawing has proved to be an effective way to communicate with the boys. When they were younger their favourite toys were included in the comics – they either give advice or learned along with the boys. Many a meltdown or hazardous situation was circumvented by a quickly drawn explanatory comic strip!

Zeke also works for a mental health charity supporting school children to develop an understanding of the importance of good mental health and providing them with a language to discuss these issues. His illustrations also support his work with refugees/asylum seekers and adults with mental health difficulties.

In recent years, Zeke has been commissioned to support delegates at a number of neurodiversity conferences –drawing graphic notes to recall their learning effectively.
In the future he hopes to publish his social stories more widely, and to continue to explore mental health and autism related issues through comic strips and animation.

Zeke too has his things!

see more of Zeke's work at www.zekeclough.co.uk

This book would not exist without the amazing support from friends, family, clients, colleagues and strangers from near and far. You made this possible
– thank you.

I would like to give particular mention to the fab folk who sent me advice, encouragement, reviews and feedback – Zoe Horne, Maria Keel, Jo Garner at ChAPS, to my especially well connected friends who suggested and recommended me to editors, experts and publishers – Natalie Gordon, Emmanuel Gobillot, Jen Wilson, to the 850+ people who have liked and shared and posted on social media @TheAspergerThing to assure me that this Thing had legs, to one particular lady who seemed to get everyone around her to buy a draft copy – Emma Romans, to the lovely Stephen Lambes who asked his children to stand in front of their class and read The Thing out loud, to my husband and children who have played the role of editors, proof readers, marketers and customers without complaint, and to anyone else I have shamelessly forgotten – you are not forgotten. ☺

A very special thank you goes to my mum – my eternal inspiration – who was the one who casually suggested "why don't you write a book?" one Monday afternoon….love you Mum x

I have an extra thank you to the wonderful people who parted with their hard earned cash to buy a signed copy before the Thing even existed: Anna Caston, Aniko Smith, Claire Bartley, Tim Brown, Chris Watkin, Dilum Jirasinghe, Marcus Downing, Hayden Pearson, Janine Rusbridge, Jerome Payne, John Field, Jen Wilson, Joanna Lay, Jo Barnard, Joe Caston, David Lees, Nadia Beauchamp, Maria Keel, Gilly Pearson, Kelly Hart, Roxy Bell, Vanessa Maguire, Zoe Franklin and Zoe Horne. Your belief in me kept me going. Thanks xx

Zeke Clough….you are a genius. Working with you has been awesome…what shall we do next?

www.ingramcontent.com/pod-product-compliance
Lightning Source LLC
Chambersburg PA
CBHW051249020426
42333CB00025B/3132